D1507271

'Twas the Season of Advent

Devotions and Stories for the Christmas Season

Written by Glenys Nellist

Illustrated by Elena Selivanova

"This book is dedicated to my eldest brother, John, whose gifts on Christmas morning were always worth waiting for. I'm proud to be your sister. Love you."
—GN

"My most sincere words of gratitude to everyone who gave me the opportunity to enjoy this marvelous story and immerse myself in the legendary times."
—ES

ZONDERKIDZ

'Twas the Season of Advent
Copyright © 2021 by Glenys Nellist
Illustrations © 2021 by Elena Selivanova

This title is also available as a Zondervan ebook.

Requests for information should be addressed to:

Zonderkidz, 3900 Sparks Dr. SE, Grand Rapids, Michigan 49546

ISBN 978-0-310-73415-4

All Scripture quotations, unless otherwise indicated, are taken from The Holy Bible, *New International Reader's Version®*, NIrV®. Copyright © 1995, 1996, 1998, 2014 by Biblica, Inc.® Used by permission of Zondervan. All rights reserved worldwide. www.Zondervan.com. The "NIrV" and "New International Reader's Version" are trademarks registered in the United States Patent and Trademark Office by Biblica, Inc.®

Any Internet addresses (websites, blogs, etc.) and telephone numbers in this book are offered as a resource. They are not intended in any way to be or imply an endorsement by Zondervan, nor does Zondervan vouch for the content of these sites and numbers for the life of this book.

All rights reserved. No part of this publication may be reproduced, stored in a retrieval system, or transmitted in any form or by any means—electronic, mechanical, photocopy, recording, or any other—except for brief quotations in printed reviews, without the prior permission of the publisher.

Zonderkidz is a trademark of Zondervan.

Editor: Mary Hassinger
Art direction and design: Cindy Davis
Printed in Malaysia

21 22 23 24 25 /IMG/ 22 21 20 19 18 17 16 15 14 13 12 11 10 9 8 7 6 5 4 3 2 1

DECEMBER 1

'Twas the season of Advent, when all through the earth,
People were pausing to ponder Christ's birth.
The bright lights were hung 'round the doorframes with care
In hopes that Christmastime soon would be there …

Welcoming Advent

Prepare the way for the LORD. —Isaiah 40:3

Welcome to the wonderful season of Advent. Do you know what Advent means? It means "the arrival of a notable person, thing, or event." Advent is a time when we wait, prepare for, and look forward to the arrival of God's Son, Jesus. But the word Advent is part of a bigger word too …

Adventure

Over the next twenty-five days, we are going to share in a wonderful adventure together. We'll begin each day in the quietness of our own homes, perhaps gathered around the Christmas tree, while all the lights are twinkling in the darkness. And we'll read together and learn about God. We'll meet angels and shepherds, magi and Mary. We'll spend time with Isaiah and Elizabeth and Joseph. And we'll end up back where we began—at the manger, where God is waiting to introduce us to Jesus. And there, at the manger, we'll worship and wonder.

Prayer
Dear God, thank you for this book we hold. Thank you for inviting us on this
wonderful adventure together, when we will draw closer to Jesus.

DECEMBER 2

And if you peeked into those houses at night,
You'd see Christmas décor—what a wonderful sight!
A tree sparkling brightly, all silver and green,
And there, in the corner, a sweet manger scene …

Come to The Manger

She gave birth to her first baby. It was a boy. She wrapped him in large strips of cloth.
Then she placed him in a manger. —Luke 2:7

ne morning, more than two thousand years ago, a carpenter in Bethlehem had a job to do. He went to his workshop and picked up his saw, a hammer, some nails, and a few pieces of wood. The carpenter whistled as he worked, and when he'd finished, he stood back to admire the manger he'd made. It was small, but strong. It would be a wonderful feeding trough for the animals.

The manger was placed in a stable and every day cows and sheep and goats would peek inside and eat their food from it. They didn't have to wait their turn. They crowded around it, because the manger held what they needed.

One special night, when Bethlehem's skies were filled with a brilliant light, God opened the gates of heaven and came down to earth. God didn't come in a blaze of fire. God didn't ride in on a gleaming chariot. God didn't march in on a mighty horse. God came quietly, in the night, like a whisper, while the world was asleep. God crept in as a tiny, helpless baby called Jesus. And the manger became his bed.

All year round, and especially during Advent, God invites us to come to the manger. God invites us to peek inside, to ponder this newborn babe who would grow up to change the world. And the beautiful thing is that we can all come to the manger—we don't have to wait our turn. There is room for everyone. There is room for you. No matter how young or old we are, no matter what we look like, or where we live, we can crowd around the manger, because the manger holds what we need: Jesus.

Prayer
Dear God, thank you for the carpenter who made the manger. Be with us this Advent,
as we wait for the wonderful day when we will celebrate the birth of Jesus.

DECEMBER 3

The story of Advent began long ago
Before there were seasons, or winter, or snow.
It began in the darkness, before day or night,
When God whispered softly, 'Let there be light.'

Let There Be Jesus

In the beginning, God created the heavens and the earth. The earth didn't have any shape. And it was empty. There was darkness over the surface of the waves. At that time, the Spirit of God was hovering over the waters. God said, "Let there be light." And there was light. —Genesis 1:1–3

n the very beginning, before the world began, there was nothing—nothing to see and nothing to hear. There was only darkness. But when God's voice spoke into the quiet and echoed into the darkness, an amazing thing happened! The world came into being. God only said four little words. But those words had the power to bring the world to life.

Let there be light.

And there was light! The Bible tells us that a wonderful light came and flooded into the darkness. The world was born.

It must have been dark in that little stable in Bethlehem too. And so quiet. It was nighttime. All the animals were sleeping. But into the quiet and into the darkness, God whispered four little words:

Let there be Jesus.

And there was Jesus! The animals woke up! A huge, bright star shone overhead, and the stable was filled with a wonderful light. When Jesus was born, light flooded into the darkness. And when Jesus grew up, he tried to shine his light of love wherever he went. He made sick people well, he loved the little children, he made friends with people who had no friends. The baby in the manger grew up to be the light of the world. Can you hear God whisper:

Let there be light.
Let there be love.
Let there be Jesus.

Prayer

Dear God, thank you for making our wonderful world and filling it with light. Thank you that when Jesus grew up, he shone the light of love wherever he went. Help us try to do that too.

DECEMBER 4

Isaiah was nestled all snug in his bed
While visions from God danced 'round in his head.
A baby was coming, God's own special Son,
To bring light from the darkness and love everyone.

Light of The World

The people who are now living in darkness will see a great light. They are now
living in a very dark land. But a light will shine on them. —Isaiah 9:2

 ave you heard of a man called Isaiah? Isaiah lived seven hundred years before Jesus was born.
But he knew that one day, Jesus would come. Isaiah was a prophet—one of God's special
messengers. And one morning God gave Isaiah a wonderful message of hope that he would
share with all the people living in Jerusalem.

Hundreds and hundreds of years before Jesus was born, all the people in the city of Jerusalem were
curled up, fast asleep in their beds—except for Isaiah. He was wide awake, standing by his open window,
watching the sun as it peeked over the horizon. Isaiah felt excited. He knew that, somehow, this wonderful
light was a special message from God.

Isaiah waited, and as the sun rose higher over the horizon its rays began to creep and dance toward the
city. At last, the sun shone over Jerusalem like a huge golden ball and all the darkness was gone. Isaiah
watched in wonder as the whole city was flooded with light and God whispered a message that made
Isaiah jump up and down. He ran to his desk, dipped his feather in ink, and hurriedly began to write on
a scroll …

A special one is coming! God's sending him our way!
It might not be tomorrow, but I know he'll come one day!
He will shine with a light that will stream from heav'n above.
He will flood the world with hope and cover it with love.

Isaiah rolled up his scroll and went back to the window. The light was still shining. Isaiah closed his eyes
and as he felt the warm sun on his face, he knew, without a doubt, that one day Jesus would be born.

Prayer
Thank you, God, for Isaiah, who listened to you all those years ago and
wrote down those words of hope that we can still read and hear today.

DECEMBER 5

After Isaiah had told the whole town,
He unrolled his scroll and wrote everything down.
Now what would the name of this special boy be?
But God whispered softly, "You must wait and see."

What Will Be His Name?

A child will be born to us. A son will be given to us. He will rule over us. And he will
be called Wonderful Adviser and Mighty God. He will also be called Father
Who Lives Forever and Prince Who Brings Peace. —Isaiah 9:6

 saiah closed his eyes and tried to imagine what the special baby would be called. Surely this child, who would one day come to earth, would have to be given a marvelous name. After all, he would be God's very own Son! His name would be greater than any other name.

Perhaps, Isaiah thought, the baby would be called Wonderful Adviser, because when he grew up, everyone in the whole world would be able to talk to him, and he would listen, and give the very best advice.

Or perhaps the baby would be called Mighty God. Wouldn't this boy grow up to be strong, powerful, and mighty? And wouldn't he be able to do impossible things?

Perhaps the baby would be called Everlasting Father, because when he grew up, he would be like the most wonderful parent in the whole world. Everyone would be part of his great family and he would be with us forever.

Or perhaps the baby would have a gentler name, like Prince of Peace, because in some wonderful and mysterious way, he'd be able to bring a peace, a quiet, and a calm into peoples' hearts that they'd never known before.

Isaiah didn't know what name would be chosen for God's Son, but he knew one thing for sure—that baby would be special. And when the time was right, God would send him to earth.

Prayer
Thank you, God, for bringing the Prince of Peace into the world and for keeping your promise to Isaiah.

DECEMBER 6

And when God was ready, an angel flew down
To a young girl named Mary, in Nazareth's town.
But she'd never seen angel, or fairy, or elf,
And she gasped when she saw him, in spite of herself.

My Answer Is Yes

The angel said to her, "Do not be afraid, Mary. God is very pleased with you. You will become pregnant and give birth to a son. You must call him Jesus. He will be great and will be called the Son of the Most High God. The Lord God will make him a king like his father David of long ago." —Luke 1:30–32

The warm scent of freshly baked bread filled the little home in Nazareth. As Mary lifted the loaves from the oven and set them aside to cool, a different scent seemed to fill the air. It was as if someone had opened the door and stepped into the room. Mary turned around and gasped in surprise. An angel was hovering, right there—right in front of her. Mary shook her head and closed her eyes. But even with her eyes shut tight, she could hear the angel softly whispering her name.

"Mary, Mary. Don't be afraid. God is with you."

Mary slowly opened her eyes and tried to make sense out of what she was seeing and hearing. The angel was bathed in soft, silvery light and its wide wings were shimmering in the early evening shadows.

"Who are you?" Mary whispered. "And why are you here?"

"I'm Gabriel," the angel answered. "And God has sent me with a special message for you. You will have a child, Mary—a son. You are to give him the name Jesus. He will be God's own Son. And he will be a king."

Mary shook her head in disbelief.

"How can that possibly be? I'm not even married yet, and I'm so young!"

"Nothing is impossible with God," Gabriel said softly. "Even Elizabeth, your relative, is going to have a baby. And everyone said she was too old. Don't worry. God will work everything out. For now, you just need to say yes."

Mary's heart skipped a beat. She could feel God's Holy Spirit dancing in the room and shining in the shadows. She looked at the angel and nodded slowly. As Gabriel faded away and flew back to heaven, Mary sank to her knees in prayer.

"I'm here, God." she whispered. "I'll do as you say. I'll be the momma of your Son. My answer is … yes."

Prayer

Dear God, thank you for Mary who was so brave and trusted you.
When I need to be brave, help me remember that you are with me.

DECEMBER 7

What the angel told Mary—how could it be true?
That she'd be a momma? Elizabeth too?
She would go to her cousin, she'd leave straight away,
And see what Elizabeth might have to say.

Elizabeth's Story

One day Zechariah … was serving as a priest in God's temple … Then an angel of the Lord appeared to Zechariah. The angel was standing at the right side of the incense altar. When Zechariah saw him, he was amazed and terrified. But the angel said to him, "Do not be afraid, Zechariah. Your prayer has been heard. Your wife Elizabeth will have a child. It will be a boy, and you must call him John." —Luke 1:8–13

lizabeth lay in her bed in the darkness and stared up at the stars outside her window. Zechariah, her husband, lay fast asleep at her side. She could hear his gentle snores. But Elizabeth couldn't sleep. She lay awake, full of wonder and joy, thinking about the day when she would hold her baby in her arms.

Smiling in the darkness, she put her hand on her tummy, and prayed for this child, this miracle, growing inside her. "Thank you, God," she whispered, "that I will be a momma."

It had been several months now since an angel had visited Zechariah while he was on duty in the temple and told him the unbelievable news—Elizabeth would have a baby. It was something they had prayed and prayed about for years. But who would have ever thought that they could have a baby now, when they were so old? But it was true! Elizabeth could feel the baby in her tummy as he kicked his legs. "We'll meet you soon, John," Elizabeth whispered.

As she closed her eyes, Elizabeth thought, for the hundredth time, about what the angel had told her husband … how her boy would be a joy and a delight, not just to her and Zechariah, but to many, many people.

The angel had said that her son would be filled with the Holy Spirit and have a special mission in life. His job would be to get people ready to meet the Lord and to prepare their hearts for him. Elizabeth didn't really know what all that meant, but it sounded like the Lord, the Messiah, the special one from God, was also going to be born soon.

As Elizabeth drifted off to sleep that night, she couldn't help wondering who the momma of the Messiah might be. Little did Elizabeth know that she was about to find out …

Prayer

Thank you, God, that you were at work in Elizabeth and Zechariah's lives.
Thank you, too, for being at work in our lives, even when we don't know it.

DECEMBER 8

As Mary set out on Ein Karem's road,
She thought about all the strange things she'd been told.
She'd never seen angels or heard them before,
And nervous, she knocked on Elizabeth's door …

A God of Impossible Things

When Elizabeth heard Mary's greeting, the baby inside her jumped. And Elizabeth was filled with the Holy Spirit. In a loud voice she called out, "God has blessed you more than other women. And blessed is the child you will have!" —Luke 1:41–42

As soon as the angel had gone back to heaven, Mary knew what she would do. She packed the things needed for her long journey and set out to visit her cousin Elizabeth. Elizabeth and Zechariah lived far away, in the little village of Ein Karem. It had been a long time since Mary had seen her relative. It would be good to see her again.

Mary knew that Elizabeth had been unhappy. All her life, Elizabeth had wanted a baby, but that baby never arrived. Her husband, Zechariah, had been praying for a child for years. But so far, his prayers had not been answered. As Mary climbed the hillside toward Elizabeth's home she couldn't help wondering how Elizabeth could have a baby when she was so old? How could Mary, herself, be carrying God's own Son inside her tummy? It all seemed so impossible. But Mary remembered the words of the angel, who had appeared to her just a few days before …

Nothing is impossible with God.

Mary walked up the little path that led to Elizabeth's home and knocked on the door. Now she would find out if what the angel had said was true. As soon as Elizabeth opened the door, Mary gasped in surprise. Immediately, she could see that her cousin was pregnant. Elizabeth put her hand on her own tummy and cried out, "Mary! What are you doing here? The baby inside me just jumped for joy! How wonderful to see the mother of my Lord!"

Mary couldn't believe what Elizabeth just said. The two women hugged and cried tears of joy. Now, Mary knew without any doubt that everything the angel had told her was true. Every. Single. Word. God could do impossible things. Elizabeth, even though she was too old, would have a baby. Mary, even though she was so young, would have a baby. And Mary's baby would be none other than God's own Son.

God does impossible things.

Prayer

Dear God, how wonderful for Mary to be able to spend time with, and talk to, her relative, Elizabeth. Thank you for our families and that we can talk to each other.

DECEMBER 9

And soon, Mary's heart was just bursting with joy,
It was true! She'd be momma of God's baby boy!
In Elizabeth's home, she sang a sweet song.
What the angel had told her was true all along.

Mary's Magnificent Song

My soul gives glory to the Lord. My spirit delights in God my Savior. He has taken note of me even though I am not considered important. From now on all people will call me blessed. The Mighty One has done great things for me. His name is holy. —Luke 1: 46–49

Mary stayed with Elizabeth for three months and every day, the two women talked about what had happened. Mary thought about the angel's visit and how blessed she was to be chosen to be the mother of God's Son. Mary couldn't really understand why God had chosen her. She was just an ordinary girl. She wasn't powerful, or rich. And no one, outside her own family, knew her name. But God did.

And one day, Mary's heart was so full of thanks and praise to God that she just couldn't hold it in, and all her joy bubbled over into song …

My spirit dances with the news,
My soul sings out for joy.
For I will be the momma
Of God's precious baby boy.

My heart is filled with gladness,
And I can't believe it's true.
That God looked down and whispered soft,
"Mary, I choose you."

I'm just an ordinary girl,
God saw me as I am.
And when I thought, "I can't do that."
God whispered, "Yes, you can."

The Mighty One, My Savior, God,
Has done great things for me.
And who knows what this child of mine
Will one day grow to be?

I only know that through the years,
In every time and place,
All people will remember
This God of love and grace.

Prayer
Dear God, thank you for the magnificent song that Mary sang to you.
Thank you for Luke, who wrote her words down so we can read them today.

DECEMBER 10

Now Joseph, the carpenter, had a strange dream.
He, too, saw an angel—now what could this mean?
But the voice of the angel, who stood by his bed,
Soon let Joseph know, he had nothing to dread.

In Love with God

The angel said, "Joseph, son of David, don't be afraid to take Mary home as your wife. The baby inside her is from the Holy Spirit. She is going to have a son. You must give him the name Jesus. That's because he will save his people from their sins." —Matthew 1: 20–22

Joseph, the carpenter, was troubled. He sanded down the last piece of cedarwood and ran his hand over the surface. It was not as smooth as it should be. The table he was making for his neighbor had to be perfect. He would have to work on it tomorrow—the evening light was fading. Joseph put his saw and hammer away and sighed as he wiped his hands with a cloth. The table he was making wasn't the only thing troubling him.

Joseph had heard a rumor about Mary, the girl he loved, the one he was soon supposed to marry. Apparently, she was going to have a baby. And Joseph wasn't the father. That could only mean one thing —Mary must be in love with someone else. Joseph's heart was heavy as he climbed into bed and lay down to sleep.

He still loved Mary. But how could he marry her now?

Joseph closed his eyes and drifted off to sleep, but in the middle of the night he thought he heard someone softly calling his name. "Joseph, Joseph."

Was that an angel hovering by his bed? "Joseph," the angel whispered. "You must marry Mary. The child inside her is God's Son. You must give him the name Jesus. Will you help take care of him?"

In the morning Joseph woke from his sleep and knew what he had to do. He would marry Mary. He would be the daddy of God's Son. He would take care of him and would teach him how to be a carpenter too.

Joseph went out to his shed, re-sanded the table from the day before, and smiled as he ran his hands over its smooth surface. One day, his son would be working in here with him. Joseph felt so happy. Now he knew—Mary wasn't in love with another man.

She was in love with God.

And that was fine … because Joseph was in love with God too

Prayer

Dear God, thank you for Joseph, an ordinary man who listened to you. Help us listen to you too.

DECEMBER 11

The angel brought good news, as all angels do,
Then straight back to heaven on silver wings flew.
But soon he'd return and fly back down to earth,
With a whole choir of angels, to sing at Christ's birth.

Angels Everywhere

Praise him, all his angels. Praise him, all his angels in heaven. —Psalm 148:2

ll through the story of Jesus's birth, from before his arrival until after he was born, we see glimpses of angels. These messengers of God winged their way down from heaven, to bring words of encouragement and hope. But how do you think you might feel if you saw an angel? The Bible tells us that Zechariah, Mary, and Joseph were all scared, but to each person, the angel said the same wonderful words:

Do not be afraid, Zechariah.

Do not be afraid, Mary.

Do not be afraid, Joseph.

And after the angels had said these encouraging words, listen to the good news they brought!

Zechariah, your prayer has been heard. Your wife Elizabeth will have a child.

Mary, God is very pleased with you.

Joseph, the baby inside Mary is from the Holy Spirit.

What wonderful words the angels brought! To Mary, in her little home; to Zechariah in the quietness of the temple; to Joseph in his warm bed—the angels came and whispered hope into human hearts.

The angels brought God's news, and that is always Good News.

Prayer
Dear God, thank you for all the angels in the Christmas story and for the good news they brought.

DECEMBER 12

Now Mary and Joseph got ready one day
To travel to Bethlehem—far, far away.
The strong little donkey climbed up hill and down
And carried tired Mary to Bethlehem town.

We've Arrived!

So Joseph … went from the town of Nazareth in Galilee to Judea. That is where Bethlehem, the town of David, was. Joseph went there because he belonged to the family line of David. He went there with Mary to be listed. —Luke 2:4–5

"Mary, are you ready?" Joseph called as he smoothed out the blanket on the little donkey's back. "We need to leave soon. We've a long journey ahead of us." Thank goodness Mary could ride on the donkey as they traveled to Bethlehem. It was seventy miles and since the baby was due any day now, it was much too far for her to walk.

"Tell me again why we have to travel to Bethlehem," Mary said, as Joseph helped her onto the donkey. She was already tired and a little worried about what lay ahead.

"It's an order from Caesar Augustus," Joseph replied. "He's taking a census, and that means we must all return to our own towns to be counted. Bethlehem is our town, Mary. It's where we're from. But don't worry. As soon as we arrive, I'll find a nice, warm inn where we can stay. And remember, God is with us."

It was true. God was watching over them—every step of the way. But it was still a huge relief to Mary when they rounded the last hill and saw the twinkling lights of Bethlehem ahead. At long last, she'd be able to get a good night's sleep. Mary put her hand on her tummy as they approached the inn.

"It's alright, Little One," she whispered. "We've arrived."

Prayer
Thank you, God, for Mary and Joseph's safe arrival in Bethlehem.

DECEMBER 13

When Joseph knocked loud on the innkeeper's door,
He told him, "I'm sorry, there's no room for more.
But I do have a stable for oxen and sheep …"
So Mary and Joseph got ready to sleep.

The Innkeeper's Tale

There was no room for them in the inn. —Luke 1:7

obias, the innkeeper, was tired. This had been the busiest night in Bethlehem ever. He had never seen so many people crowding into the little town, all looking for somewhere to stay so they could be counted for the census tomorrow. Every room in his inn was full.

Just as Tobias was getting ready to lock up for the night, there came a loud knock on his door. "I'm so sorry," he started to say, as he opened the door. But before he could finish his sentence, Joseph pleaded with him. "Sir, if you have anywhere at all where we could stay, we would be so grateful. My wife is about to have her baby. Please, can you help?"

Tobias scratched his beard. He looked at the young girl, sitting on a donkey. She looked so tired. He did have a small stable. It was full of animals, but at least it would be warm. Tobias got his candle and led Mary and Joseph to the stable. All the animals were snoozing and looked up in surprise as the door opened and Mary and Joseph went inside.

As Tobias turned away to go back to his inn, he had the strangest feeling about that little stable—it felt different that night … like it was a holy place, like they were all waiting for something to happen, like heaven was about to come down to earth …

Prayer
Dear God, thank you so much for the innkeeper who was willing to help Mary
and Joseph that night. Open our eyes and hearts to be willing to help others in need.

DECEMBER 14

Bethlehem lies sleeping, beneath a silver moon,
Waiting for a baby—his birth is coming soon.
A star shines in the darkness, heaven's silent sign.
Bethlehem lies sleeping—this is waiting time.

Waiting Time

It is good when people wait quietly for the Lord to save them. —Lamentations 3:25–27

If you've ever been to the theater to see a play, you'll know that the story is acted out on a big stage. Halfway through, there's a pause, or an interval or intermission A curtain is drawn across the stage and people wait for the second half to begin. That's where we are now, in our Advent journey. We're halfway to Christmas day. But as we wait, we can wonder; and as we pause, we can ponder. We can think about the story, about what's happened so far, and what will happen next.
Waiting time becomes wondering time …

I wonder if Joseph knew that the baby would be born this night …

I wonder how Mary felt about sleeping in a stable …

I wonder why Jesus was born in a stable …

I wonder where God was this night …

Prayer
Dear God, thank you for this Advent journey we're on. Thank you that you
meet us here, in the stillness of our homes and in the quietness of our hearts.

DECEMBER 15

It was dark in the stable—the cows and the sheep,
The donkey and oxen were all fast asleep.
When during the night there arose such a clatter,
They sprang from their naps to see what was the matter.

No Room?

While Joseph and Mary were there, the time came for the child to be born.
She gave birth to her first baby. It was a boy. —Luke 2:6–7

t was dark in Bethlehem's little stable. The cows were curled up in the corner, the sheep were snoozing in the shadows, and the donkey was dozing in the darkness. Nighttime in the stable was usually a quiet affair. But not this night. This night was different …

It was in the early hours of the morning, long before the sun rose, when the piercing cries of a newborn baby filled the air and jolted all the animals awake. The sheep, donkey, pigeons, and the mouse in the manger were all amazed at what had just happened. A baby had been born in their stable! The stable had been birthplace for lots of baby animals, but never before had a real human baby made its arrival here.

The cows and the sheep ambled over to see the newborn baby. The pigeons peeked down from the rafters above and the mouse in the manger stood on tiptoes to get a better look. His whiskers quivered with excitement. It was a boy! His momma was holding him tight and his dad was so proud!

Outside the window, there was the biggest, brightest star the mouse had ever seen. It seemed to flood the whole stable with light. And was that some sort of music the mouse could hear? Where was that coming from? It sounded like bells ringing way up high in the sky.

What an amazing night! the little mouse thought to himself as he snuggled back down in his comfy bed in the manger.

It was later that evening when the little mouse woke up, surprised to see Mary standing over the manger. Her baby was fast asleep, and as Mary bent down to place him in the manger, the little mouse hid under the hay. He was worried. Would there really be room in here for this baby?

The little mouse waited a while, and when he was sure that Mary and Joseph were fast asleep, he crept out from his hiding place and tiptoed up to the baby boy. And as he peered into the face of this sleeping child, the little mouse knew, in his heart, there would always be room for this baby.

Prayer
Thank you, God, for the night Jesus was born, even though it was in a stable. Help us to appreciate what we have, including our warm homes and comfy beds.

DECEMBER 16

And there, in the corner, a new baby boy
Was crying out loud, as his dad smiled with joy.
His mom wrapped her baby in cloth strips of white
And sang a sweet lullaby, holding him tight.

Your Name is Jesus

She wrapped him in large strips of cloth. Then she placed him in a manger. —Luke 2:7

ary wrapped her baby in strips of white cloth and rocked him gently back and forth. The stable filled with the soft sounds of her lullaby until the baby closed his eyes and fell fast asleep. Mary looked down at his tiny hands and his little eyelashes resting on those baby cheeks. Her boy was perfect!

"Jesus," she whispered in the darkness. "Your name is Jesus."

Joseph nodded as he remembered the words of the angel who had appeared in his dream several months before … *You must give him the name Jesus. That's because he will save his people from their sins.*

But what did that mean? Jesus was just a tiny, helpless baby. Even when he grew up, how was he going to be able to save people from their sins?

Mary closed her eyes as she, too, remembered what the angel had said to her …

You must call him Jesus. He will be great and will be called the Son of the Most High God. The Lord God will make him a king like his father David of long ago.

Her son would be a king? So would he wear a crown? Mary couldn't believe it. It didn't make sense. Here she was, holding her newborn son, in this smelly stable, where all the animals lay asleep around her. What kind of king would be born in a place like this? Wasn't a king supposed to be born in a big, shiny palace, or in a grand city, like Jerusalem? Surely a king wouldn't be born in a small, humble stable in a little town like Bethlehem? But Mary believed the angel's words. They had touched her somewhere deep inside and spoken to her heart. Her boy would be great. He would be called Son of the Most High God, and even though it seemed unbelievable, Jesus would be a king.

Mary kissed Jesus good night and laid him in the manger. "I'm so glad to be your momma," she whispered to him in the darkness. "Whatever happens in your life, and whatever you grow up to be, I'll always be your momma."

Prayer
Thank you, God, for the gift of life and families; for Jesus and Mary and Joseph.

DECEMBER 17

From high up in heaven came sweet singing too,
As everything told by Isaiah came true.
Immanuel lay in a manger so small,
Our God had come down to be with us all.

Immanuel

She will give birth to a son. And he will be called Immanuel.
The name Immanuel means "God with us." —Matthew 1:23

even hundred years had passed since Isaiah ran through the streets of Jerusalem, bringing news of a special baby boy who would come into the world. And on that Bethlehem night, Isaiah's words came true. Here, lying in the manger was the:

Wonderful Adviser
Mighty God
Everlasting Father
Prince of Peace

But did you know that Isaiah also wrote down one more name? It was the name Immanuel, which means, God with us.

Immanuel is a beautiful name for Jesus. It means that God came down to earth, in human form, to live with us and talk with us, to cry with us and walk with us. And that is what Jesus did. When that baby in the manger grew up, he lived in Israel. Jesus talked to everyone he met, whether they were young or old, women or men. When people came to him with questions, he listened. He taught people how to pray and told them everything he knew about God. Jesus cried with two sisters when their brother died, and he walked with twelve disciples on the roads in Galilee and Jerusalem.

And the most wonderful part of Immanuel's story is that even after Jesus died, God was still with us. God sent the Holy Spirit to be with us every second of every single day. And that means no matter how we feel, God is with us. When we are happy, God is with us.

When we are sad, God is with us. When we play, or laugh, or cry, or question, God is with us.

No matter how we feel or where we go, God is always with us. Immanuel is with us.

Prayer

Dear God, even though you are invisible, we know that you are with us every second of every day, no matter where we are, no matter how we feel. Help us to remember that.

DECEMBER 18

In Bethlehem's fields, not too far away,
The shepherds were resting from their busy day.
As darkness came creeping, a light filled the sky
And a whole choir of angels appeared way up high.

Bethlehem's Fields

There were shepherds living out in the fields nearby. It was night,
and they were taking care of their sheep. —Luke 2:8

o you know who the very first people were to hear the news of Immanuel's birth? Since a new king had just been born, you might think that all the important people in Bethlehem would be told first. After all, when a royal prince or princess is born today, the news is given to all the important people in the government first, before anyone else finds out.

But when Jesus was born, some very ordinary people were the first to be told. The wonderful news of his arrival came to shepherds first. On that holy night, the shepherds in Bethlehem's fields were watching over their sheep, just like every other night, when something truly amazing happened. The royal birth announcement came from heaven itself! What a wonderful privilege for those shepherds, whose days were so ordinary.

A day in the life of a shepherd in Bethlehem was a busy one. His job was to take care of his sheep. Every day, early in the morning, he would wake them, and together they would set off, up and down the hillsides, in search of the greenest grass and the cleanest water. The shepherd would always be in the lead and his sheep would follow behind. If any baby lambs got tired on the way, he would pick them up and carry them on his shoulders. If any of his sheep got stuck on the hillside, the shepherd would gently hook his staff around their neck and carefully lift them to safety.

At night, before darkness fell, the shepherd would count all his sheep, lead them safely back to the fold, and lie down with them. But he wouldn't go to sleep. Nighttime could be dangerous. Once it was dark, a shepherd had to be careful. Wolves or bears or mountain lions could sneak up and snatch one of the sheep away. A shepherd wouldn't really expect anything good to happen at night.

But on the night Jesus was born, something utterly amazing happened in the darkness. Those ordinary shepherds were about to hear the most wonderful news in the world. Just when they least expected it, good news was about to come …

Prayer

Dear God, thank you that you watch over each one of us, just like a shepherd watches over his sheep.

DECEMBER 19

And the angels sang, 'Shepherds, please do what we say.
You must gather your sheep and leave, straight away!
To Bethlehem town, to a stable so small,
Now dash away, dash away, dash away, all!"

Good News!

An angel of the Lord appeared to them. And the glory of the Lord shone around them.
They were terrified. But the angel said to them, "Do not be afraid. I bring you good news. It will
bring great joy for all the people. Today in the town of David a Savior has been born to you.
He is the Messiah, the Lord." —Luke 2: 9–12

Skies were clear in Bethlehem that night. In the fields not too far from the stable, the shepherds settled down for the evening. They huddled together with their sheep, watching carefully in case any dangers lurked in the shadows. In the light of the silver moon they could see the little lambs nestled close by their mothers. All was quiet.

Suddenly the biggest, brightest light the shepherds had ever seen flooded the sky above. They jumped to their feet in alarm and covered their eyes as they tried to make out what was happening. The shepherds stared in amazement and trembled in fear as an angel appeared above them. But the words the angel spoke were the most incredible words the shepherds had ever heard.

Shepherds, do not be afraid! We bring only good news! This very day, the Savior of the World has been born in Bethlehem. You'll find him wrapped in cloths of white, lying in a manger. Go and see for yourselves!

And just then, the sky grew brighter as a whole choir of angels flew down from heaven and started to sing:

Glory to God in highest heaven! Peace be upon the earth!

It was the most wonderful choir the shepherds had ever heard. The shepherds knew exactly what to do. They scrambled to their feet, picked up the lambs, and set off running for Bethlehem. And if you'd been with them that night, you would have heard them talking as they ran …

How amazing was that!
How come the angels appeared to us?
Do you think it's all true?

The shepherds were about to find out.

Prayer
Thank you, God, for sending your angels to those ordinary shepherds with such amazing news.

DECEMBER 20

As soon as the shepherds had heard the good news
They ran to the stable—they'd no time to lose.
It was true, every word that the angel had said.
They found Jesus asleep in his sweet manger-bed.

The Night the Angels Came Down

So they hurried off and found Mary and Joseph and the baby. The baby was lying in the manger. After the shepherds had seen him, they told everyone. They reported what the angel had said about this child. All who heard it were amazed at what the shepherds said to them. —Luke 2: 16–18

Hannah, the young shepherd girl, couldn't believe what she'd just seen and heard. She stood, gazing into the dark skies as the angels faded away and flew back to heaven. This was unbelievable! "Hannah! Let's go!" her dad shouted, as he picked up two of the little lambs and tucked one under each arm. "Let's see if what the angels said is really true!"

Hannah grabbed another lamb and set off running for Bethlehem. And as she ran along, under the silver moon, she thought about how those angels had sung like a heavenly choir in the darkness, how they'd hovered over her head with glittering wings, and how amazing their words had been … *Do not be afraid! We bring only good news! This very day, the Savior of the World has been born … go and see for yourselves!*

Would they really find a baby wrapped in cloths, lying in a manger?

When Hannah and her dad reached the stable, they paused and waited for the rest of the shepherds to arrive. And as they waited, Hannah looked up at the twinkling stars above Bethlehem and knew, deep inside, that this was a special night.

When all the shepherds had arrived at the stable, Hannah pushed open the door and gasped at what she saw. It was all true! Mary and Joseph smiled as Hannah crept toward the manger, knelt down, and gazed at their little one. Here he was, the Savior of the World, lying in the hay.

As the baby slept, a light came from his face, and Hannah felt a peace that filled the whole stable. And Hannah knew then, as she looked at that sleeping baby, that she was looking at the face of God.

The shepherds stayed for a long time. And as they ran back to the fields, they told everyone about what they had seen and heard. Hannah never forgot that night. It was the night she saw the face of God, the night when the angels came down, and the night when the Savior of the World came down too.

Prayer
Thank you, God, for shepherds, and angels, and good news that came in the dark.

DECEMBER 21

Now a long way away lived three magi, or kings,
Who were scanning the skies for beautiful things.
When what to their wondering eyes should appear,
But a star in the east, shining bold, bright, and clear.

Journey of The Magi

After Jesus was born in Bethlehem in Judea, during the time of King Herod, Magi from the east came to Jerusalem and asked, "Where is the one who has been born King of the Jews? We saw his star when it rose and have come to worship him." … The star they had seen when it rose went ahead of them until it stopped over the place where the child was. When they saw the star, they were overjoyed.
—Matthew 2: 1–3; 9–10

In the far-away land of Persia, three wise men stood in the tent, poring over their carefully drawn chart of the night skies. "If our measurements are correct," said the first, as he tapped the chart with his finger, "that huge star is directly above Israel, somewhere near a town called Bethlehem."

"Then that's where we'll find the king," the second one whispered, his eyes shining with excitement.

The three wise men went outside and squinted into the dark skies above. There it was—the biggest, brightest star the astrologers had ever seen, shining in the east. "We leave tomorrow," the third one said.

It was thousands of miles from Persia to Bethlehem. The three wise men traveled through the hot, sandy desert, resting during the day and riding through the night, following the star as it led them on their way. And finally, they came to the place where Jesus was. At long last, after waiting many years and traveling thousands of miles, they were standing on the threshold of meeting the Promised One.

At the loud knock, Joseph opened the door and was amazed to see three men, splendidly dressed, standing in front of him. "Where is our King?" the wise men asked, as they bowed low to the ground.

"For we have come to worship him."

Prayer
Thank you, God, for the three wise men who traveled all those long miles to worship Jesus.

DECEMBER 22

"Let's find the new King!" the three magi cried,
As they jumped on their camels and started to ride.
And they knelt before Jesus with gifts to behold,
As Mary remembered the things she'd been told.

Gifts for a King

On coming to the house, they saw the child with his mother Mary, and they bowed
down and worshiped him. Then they opened their treasures and presented him
with gifts of gold, frankincense and myrrh. —Matthew 2:11

ary, there's someone here to see Jesus," Joseph said, as he ushered the visitors into the room.
Mary was sitting by the window with her son on her lap and she looked up in surprise to see
three men who looked like kings standing in the doorway. Each one was holding a shiny,
precious gift and their splendid robes swished on the floor as they walked toward her.

"We are here to worship the King," said the first. As he knelt in front of Jesus, Mary marveled at his
purple cloak and the sparkling jewels in his crown. "I bring gold for the King," he said softly as he placed
a glittering vessel on the ground in front of Jesus. Mary looked at the gold and remembered then, the angel
Gabriel's visit. It seemed like a long time ago now, but Mary could still hear his words … The Lord God
will make him a King

"And I bring frankincense," the second one said, as he carried a bejeweled jar towards Jesus. Mary couldn't
help noticing his fur-lined cloak and the glittering rings adorning his fingers as he placed his gift on the
floor. "This incense is a sign of our worship," he said.

Mary looked at the incense and remembered, then, how incense was used by the priests in the temple as
they worshiped God.

"And I bring myrrh, an expensive perfume," the third one said softly, as he knelt and placed a golden urn
before Jesus. "Thank you," said Mary quietly, as the wise man looked deep into her eyes. The room was
silent.

Later that night, after the three wise men were long gone, Mary stood by her window and looked at the
bright, shining star that had led them to her son. She swayed gently back and forth, as she lulled Jesus
to sleep on her shoulder.

And in the corner of the room, in the light of the star, sat three shining gifts of gold, frankincense,
and myrrh.

Prayer

Dear God, thank you for the gifts that the wise men brought to Jesus.
Thank you for the gifts that we will give and receive this Christmas.

DECEMBER 23

She treasured the memories stored up in her heart …
Of shepherds and angels, and how, from the start,
She'd promised to love and to care for God's Son,
This Jesus, Immanuel, the Mighty One.

Treasure Up These Things

But Mary kept all these things like a secret treasure in her heart.
She thought about them over and over. —Luke 2:19

If Mary had owned a treasure box where she could store her precious memories, what do you think would be inside? If photography had been invented all those years ago, Mary's treasure box might contain photographs of the angel Gabriel, of her and Elizabeth standing together, of the donkey that carried her to Bethlehem, the happy couple smiling with their brand-new baby boy, a group of shepherds gazing at the new arrival, and a trio of wise men dressed in finery. But even if photography had been invented, Mary didn't need a treasure box, because she stored all those precious memories in her heart.

In Mary's heart, she kept all her memories safe—of how the angel Gabriel had brought the amazing news, her precious time spent with Elizabeth, the long, hard journey to Bethlehem, and the wonderful night when Jesus was born. Mary would never forget the visit from the shepherds who had rushed to the stable that night, and how, later, those three wise men had brought splendid gifts and knelt in front of her son.

Mary thought back over everything that had happened—all the people she'd met, all the places she'd visited, and all the words she'd heard. And she thought deeply about each moment and what it all might mean.

We are almost at the end of our Advent journey. It's a good time for us to pause and 'treasure up' all the things we've seen and heard. We've visited many places together through these pages—we've traveled to Jerusalem with Isaiah, to Nazareth with the angel Gabriel, and we've walked to Ein Karem with Mary. We've journeyed to Bethlehem on a donkey and ridden on camels across the desert with three wise men.

We've met some wonderful people too. Beginning with the prophet Isaiah, we've spent time with Mary and Elizabeth, Joseph and the angel Gabriel. We've encountered the innkeeper in Bethlehem, a choir of angels in the sky, shepherds in the fields, and three magnificent magi who worshiped the King.

The stories of all the places we've visited and all the people we've met are woven together to create one big story. But this story isn't finished yet. The day Jesus came to earth was really only the beginning. The story of Jesus continues through you. You can be part of the Christmas story as you worship Jesus, like the wise men, and spread the good news about his birth, like the shepherds.

You can be part of the most wonderful story in the world.

Prayer
Help me, God, to be part of the Christmas story as I worship Jesus and tell others about him.

DECEMBER 24

And after the wise men had made their way home,
Leaving Mary and Joseph and Jesus alone,
The star still shone brightly from heaven above
And bathed this new family in God's grace and love.

The First Christmas Eve

The Word became a human being. He made his home with us. We have seen his glory. It is the glory of the One and Only … And the Word was full of grace and truth. —John 1:14

On that first Christmas Eve all those years ago a young couple traveled to Bethlehem. They didn't know that the baby Mary carried inside her would be born in a stable the next day. They never knew that over two thousand years later, people all over the world would be celebrating his birth, or that this special time would be called Christmas. Mary and Joseph only knew that they had been chosen to be the earthly parents of God's Son and whatever happened, God would be in all the details. Mary and Joseph's wonderful, faithful story is what we remember on this holy night that we call Christmas Eve.

For many, many people all around the world, this is a very busy night too. Some people may be shopping for last-minute gifts; others will be wrapping them and placing them under the tree.

Kitchens will be bustling with food preparations; families will be baking and decorating cookies together; some will make mince pies. Others will prepare hams or turkeys or other special foods to be enjoyed.

Some families will jump in their cars and journey across town to be with relatives this night. They will eat together around the dinner table and tell stories and swap gifts. And others will wait until tomorrow before giving and receiving them.

On this Christmas Eve, many driveways and sidewalks will be lined with hundreds of little candles that twinkle in the darkness. Churches will be full, candles will be lit, and choirs will sing as people all over the world prepare to celebrate the birth of Jesus.

I wonder how you are celebrating this holy night. I hope that wherever you are, whatever you're doing, you might come to the manger, where God is waiting to meet you. No matter if your home is quiet or noisy this Christmas Eve—in the hustle or the hush; in the chaos or the calm; in the sound or in the silence, God is waiting to meet you there.

Prayer

*Dear God, as we gather around the manger, help us to listen as you whisper into
our hearts. Help each one of us truly know that this child—Jesus, Prince of Peace,
Immanuel, the Word, was born for us. Thank you for this holy Christmas Eve.*

DECEMBER 25

Happy Birthday, Jesus!

As Mary and Joseph stood under the star,
And thought about Jesus and things from afar,
They heard a God-whisper, that danced through the light …

Merry Christmas to all, and to all, a good night.